Crazy About

HORSES

Everything HORSE LOVERS Need to Know

by Molly Kolpin and Donna Bowman Bratton

CAPSTONE PRESS
a capstone imprint

TABLE *of* CONTENTS

CHAPTER 3
Saddle Up

CHAPTER 4
Horse Care

All About
HORSES

Horses RULE. Dogs DROOL!

If a dog is man's best friend, then for girls this honor goes to the horse. With their large, intelligent eyes and curious, loyal natures, horses make excellent companions. Sure a horse can't sit on your lap. But horse-loving girls can't imagine anything better than exploring a trail or galloping through the countryside on horseback. Ride through life with a horse at your side (or under your saddle), and you're in for an incredible adventure.

ARE YOU HORSE OBSESSED?

1. Your favorite shoes to shop for are:
   a. riding boots
   b. sneakers
   c. sandals

2. Your ideal vacation would take place:
   a. at a horse ranch
   b. on a tropical island
   c. in a big city

3. When you grow up, you want to be:
   a. a riding instructor
   b. a doctor
   c. a fashion designer

4. At the library, you most often check out books from this series:
   a. *The Saddle Club* by Bonnie Bryant
   b. *The Baby-Sitters Club* by Ann M. Martin
   c. *Harry Potter* by J.K. Rowling

5. You would wait in line for hours to get tickets to:
   a. the Kentucky Derby
   b. a Justin Bieber concert
   c. a movie premiere

6. Your favorite sport to watch is:
   a. polo
   b. gymnastics
   c. tennis

7. You know that jodhpurs are:
   a. riding pants
   b. handheld electronic gadgets
   c. tiny bugs that look like miniature butterflies

8. Your favorite way to spend a Saturday would be:
   a. horseback riding
   b. shopping
   c. painting

If all of your answers are "a," you're officially horse obsessed!

A rider who sits sidesaddle has both legs on one side of the horse.

DID YOU KNOW?

For many centuries it was considered unladylike for girls to sit astride a horse. Instead they had to ride sidesaddle.

SAFETY FIRST!

Never approach a horse without permission or adult supervision. Not all of these animals are gentle giants!

A Gallop through History

Sixty million years ago, horses began to develop in the southeastern area of North America. The horse's earliest ancestors were little larger than rabbits. They ran on feet with toes and filled their bellies with leaves. They looked a bit like small foxes with long necks.

Slowly these animals spread to other continents and transformed into modern-day horses. Their toed feet turned into hooves, and they began to eat grass instead of leaves. Most noticeably their size grew until they became the big, powerful animals you know today.

The dawn horse was a prehistoric ancestor of modern horses. It roamed North America and Europe about 55 million years ago.

GROWING PAINS

The horse's transformation over time was filled with twists and turns. It wasn't a tidy, straightforward process. Many strange-looking animals separate today's horse from its earliest ancestors.

DID YOU KNOW?

Horses are part of the scientific group called Equus. This group also includes zebras and donkeys.

TIP to TAIL

Horses' flowing manes and shiny coats have won over countless admirers. But their looks have more to do with practicality than prettiness. When living in the wild, horses needed to be able to outrun dangerous predators, such as wolves and mountain lions. They developed strong, muscular legs to help them sprint. Narrow faces and bodies reduce wind resistance and help horses maintain high speeds when galloping.

Not every feature on a horse was designed for speed, however. A horse's long neck lets it graze for grass. Its swishy tail helps it swat at pesky flies. All these practical qualities result in a gorgeous animal!

HAND IT TO THE HORSE!

In the early days, people measured horses with their hands. Over time more precise ways to measure horses were developed, but the term "hand" stuck. One hand represents 4 inches (10 centimeters). Height is measured from a horse's hooves to the top of its withers.

DID YOU KNOW?

Horses can lock their rear legs in place, which allows them to sleep while standing.

Coat Colors

When most girls think of horses, the colors black or brown come to mind. But horse coats actually include a wide variety of colors. Dapple gray, for example, is a gray coat with darker-colored rings. A gray coat with brown flecks is called fleabitten. Strawberry-roan is chestnut and white, while blue roan is black or brown with white. Bay refers to a horse with a solid-colored coat and a black mane, tail, and legs.

The list goes on and on. Add spots and patches to the mix, and it's easy to see why horse coloring is a complicated topic!

bay

COMMON FACIAL MARKINGS

bald face

blaze

star

snip

Sensible Steeds

Like people, horses experience the world through their five senses. Large eyes on the sides of their heads allow horses to see in almost all directions. On a windy day, horses can take in scents from up to 1 mile (1.6 kilometers) away. Horses also pick up on sounds carried by the wind. They twist their ears in all directions to pinpoint noises.

Because horses have taste buds, their sense of taste is very similar to humans. But this animal has a special trick when it comes to touch. Not only do horses feel through their skin, but they also feel through extra-sensitive whiskers on their muzzles.

DID YOU KNOW?
Horses have larger eyes than any other land mammal.

HORSE VS. HUMAN

Horses have the same five senses you do,
but they use their senses differently.

1. Horses can see _____ colors than humans.

a. more   **b.** fewer

2. Horses can hear _____ noises that humans can't.

a. low-pitched   **b.** high-pitched
c. faraway   **d.** all of the above

3. Both horses and humans can taste _____.

a. sweet   **b.** salty
c. sour   **d.** bitter
e. all of the above

4. Unlike humans, horses have a special body part called the _____ that helps them smell.

a. nostril aid   **b.** scent detector
c. Jacobson's organ

5. Horses have tough skin, but they're sensitive to touch like humans thanks to countless _____.

a. nerve endings
b. feeler fingers
c. touch entrappers

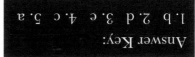
Answer Key:
1.b 2.d 3.e 4.c 5.a

15

A Neighborly CHAT

Horses communicate with each other through their own special language. Humans have no way of knowing for sure how horse-speak translates into language. But careful observations have led to some pretty good guesses.

When a horse neighs, it's usually checking in with another horse or greeting its owner. Sometimes horses make rumbling sounds called nickers. This can be interpreted as a friendly hello. Watch out for the not-so-friendly roar. A horse that makes this sound is usually angry!

GIRL POWER!

Wild horse herds have their own leader system. A male is in charge of protecting the herd. But the herd's decision-maker is a female. This older female is in charge of locating food, water, and shelter for the group. She also disciplines the younger horses and even leads the herd when running from predators.

DID YOU KNOW?

"Whinny" is another term for "neigh."

Equine Signs

Horses don't always use noises to communicate. In fact most of their communication happens through body language. They use their ears, eyes, hooves, and tails to show how they're feeling.

A horse perks up its ears and points them forward when it's alert and ready to go. When it's angry, it will pin its ears back flat against its head. If a horse is relaxed, chances are its tail will be relaxed. But if a horse is crabby, its tail will be stiff or switching back and forth. A horse that stamps its hooves is probably cranky. Be especially careful if a horse is stamping its hooves with wide eyes and flared nostrils. This could be a sign the horse is ready to kick!

KEEP YOUR EYES ON THE EARS!

Read a horse's mood at a glance by memorizing these common ear signals.

alert

ears are up and face forward

relaxed or sleepy

ears point sideways

angry

ears are pinned back

DID YOU KNOW?

Sometimes horses communicate by rearing up on their hind legs. This action is usually done to scare an enemy.

EARLY *Days*

Newborn horses called foals are usually born in the spring. A foal's size can vary, depending on the breed. The foal stands up on its long, thin legs within its first hour of life. Before a day passes, it can both walk and run.

Just because a foal moves like an adult horse doesn't mean it looks like one. Instead of smooth, shiny coats, foals are covered in soft, fluffy coats. Their legs are long for their bodies. They have short tails and thin, wispy manes that stick straight up. It takes about four months before foals start to look like adults. At 6 months old, a foal is ready to leave its mother and live life on its own.

DID YOU KNOW?
Horses can live to be 25 years old or older.

foal—a young horse (under 1 year old) that drinks its mother's milk

weanling—a young horse (about 6 months to 1 year of age) that has stopped drinking its mother's milk

yearling—a horse between 1 and 2 years old

filly—a female horse that's less than 4 years old
colt—a male horse that's less than 4 years old

mare—a female horse that's at least 4 years old

stallion—a male horse that's at least 4 years old and can be used for breeding

Learning the Ropes

Horses are adults when they're 4 years old. But horses that will carry riders have a lot to learn before reaching adulthood. First they must get used to people. Good trainers will start handling young horses right away. The trainer should have positive interactions with the horse so it bonds with humans. For example, safely handling a horse's hoof can build trust. Through positive and safe interactions, horses can learn to be calm around people. These processes are called gentling. Gentling can take a year or more, depending on the horse.

Horses should be introduced to riding equipment when they are yearlings. By the age of 2 or 3, most horses are ready to carry their first riders. Only experienced riders should handle young horses.

TRAINING LEGS

A horse's legs aren't fully developed until it's 1 or 2 years old. If a horse is exercised for too long before it reaches this age, it may become injured. Make sure a horse can safely carry a person's weight before riding it.

DID YOU KNOW?

Some racehorses begin their careers at just 2 years old.

23

HORSES
Then AND *Now*

Horses and humans have worked as teams for thousands of years. Originally horses were used to herd sheep and cattle. But people quickly realized horses could help them in other ways as well. They used horses as a means of transportation and also to carry warriors into battle.

Today vehicles and machines have replaced many of the horse's traditional jobs. But in North America and Australia, some horses are still used to herd livestock. Cowboys in the western United States, for instance, ride horses when roping cattle. A steady horse will follow the cow and let its rider focus on roping the animal. Horses are also still used to pull loads through thick forests where vehicles can't easily drive.

A HORSE ON THE FORCE!

One of the modern-day horse's most important jobs is to help the police. Big-city police forces use horses to carry officers through crowded streets. Officers on horseback have a better view of crowds than they do on foot.

DID YOU KNOW?

Humans first started working with horses around 5,000 years ago.

Giddy Up!

Few horse lovers can resist an opportunity to hop in the saddle and explore a trail. But hold your horses! Before riding into the sunset, it's important to learn about riding equipment.

To stay comfortable riders sit on a saddle and put their feet through stirrups. A rider uses reins to tell the horse where to go. Reins are attached to a bit, which goes in the horse's mouth. When a rider moves the reins, pressure is put on the bit. This tells the horse to turn or slow down. Horses should also wear horseshoes to protect their hooves from rough roads or trails.

RIDING RULES

A rider should always wear boots and a protective helmet. Boots should have heels so feet won't slip through the stirrups. (If a rider falls and gets a foot stuck in the stirrup, he or she could be dragged and badly injured.) Also make sure the helmet is meant for horseback riding. Bike helmets aren't designed to protect riders from horse accidents.

DID YOU KNOW?

Horse riding is great exercise. But remember young riders should always ride with an adult present.

Horse Hobbies

Though horses have fewer jobs than in the past, they remain as popular as ever. Instead of putting horses to work, people now use them for recreation. Horse competitions such as show jumping and dressage have become popular in recent years.

Horse enthusiasts especially love watching racehorses sprint around a track. Famous races such as the Kentucky Derby draw millions of viewers each year. Some horses have even become famous entertainers, such as Bamboo Harvester. Bamboo Harvester played the talking horse on the 1960s' TV show *Mister Ed*. Horses have even starred in popular films such as *Secretariat* and *Dreamer*.

Bamboo Harvester

DID YOU KNOW?

Bamboo Harvester starred on *Mister Ed* from 1961 to 1966.

NO HORSE? NO PROBLEM.

Satisfy your horse obsession by:
- Joining an organization, such as 4-H
- Volunteering at a stable, zoo, or farm
- Reading books such as *The Saddle Club* by Bonnie Bryant or the *Thoroughbred* series by Joanna Campbell
- Watching horse movies, such as *Black Beauty* and *Secretariat*

DID YOU KNOW?

When you volunteer at a stable, you may be asked to clean out stalls, or feed and groom horses.

Favorite HORSES

BREED *Basics*

From the Appaloosa's colorful coat to the Clydesdale's incredible strength, every horse breed has its own claim to fame. Surprisingly most modern-day horse breeds' unique features did not happen by accident. Humans created different horse breeds for specific reasons. Some horses were bred to move at breathtaking speeds. Others were bred to help farmers and cattle ranchers with their work.

To the untrained eye, it can be difficult to tell different horse breeds apart. But horse-loving girls make it their mission to know every feature of their favorite breeds.

WHICH BREED IS BEST?

When choosing a horse, it's important to pick a breed that fits the owner's needs. See what breed you'd pick by filling in the blanks below.

Appaloosa

I love horses that are _____ .
a. strong   **b.** fast   **c.** versatile
My ideal horse would be able to _____ .
a. pull heavy loads   **b.** race
c. go on trail rides
Horses that _____ are my favorite.
a. are very large
b. have fiery temperaments
c. need to be trained to carry riders

If your answers were mostly "a," a Percheron or Clydesdale is best for you. If you answered mostly "b," a Thoroughbred is your breed. If your answers were mostly "c," your best match is probably a quarter horse, Morgan, Appaloosa, or paint horse.

Thoroughbred

WHERE IT ALL BEGAN

Arabian

The world's oldest breed of horse is the Arabian. This striking horse is the source of all other breeds. The Bedouins of the Arabian Desert developed the breed centuries ago. They needed a horse with stamina to carry them across the desert plains. Arabians are now renowned throughout the world for their strength, endurance, intelligence, beauty, and gentle natures.

HORSES GALORE

More than 100 different horse breeds exist today. They are divided into three main groups—heavy horses, light horses, and ponies. Some people believe ponies are baby horses, but this is not true. Ponies are a type of small horse with long, broad bodies and thick coats.

All-AMERICAN Classics

Today the United States is home to more horses than any other country in the world. But horse numbers weren't always so high. Scientists believe the horse's earliest ancestors originated in North America and then spread to other continents. Over time all the prehistoric horses in America eventually died out. Then in the 1700s, Spanish explorers reintroduced horses to America. The small, robust horses they brought over on ships were called Colonial Spanish horses.

It wasn't long before horses became an important part of American culture. American Indians rode horses when hunting buffalo. Western cowboys rode horses when herding and roping cattle. Soldiers even rode horses into battle during times of war. Over the years dedicated horse lovers developed their own all-American breeds.

HORSES ON THE MOVE

Wondering how America's earliest horses made it across the ocean to Europe and Asia? Here's a hint—they didn't swim. Instead they crossed what is now known as the Bering Strait. Millions of years ago, this area of water between Alaska and Russia didn't exist. The two landmasses were connected, and horses simply walked across!

DID YOU KNOW?

America's wild mustangs descend from the horses brought over by Spanish explorers.

mustang

Quarter HORSE

Strong, sturdy, smart, and fast, the quarter horse is recognized as the world's most popular breed. These horses stand about 15 to 16 hands high. Their muscular frames contain large quarters that give the horses their speed. But don't think the name quarter horse comes from their giant quarters. The name actually refers to the quarter-mile races these horses once participated in. Quarter horses can reach speeds up to 55 miles (89 km) per hour when sprinting!

There are still a few quarter-mile races held in the United States today. But today quarter horses are known more for their herding skills than for their short-distance sprinting abilities. Their agility and control, combined with their intelligence, make them ideal horses for roping cattle. They quickly became the favorite breed of countless cowboys and cowgirls working on the Western frontier.

BREED BEGINNINGS

The quarter horse isn't just the most popular American horse breed. It's also the oldest. Early settlers began developing the quarter horse in the 1600s. They bred both English and Spanish horses to create the breed.

DID YOU KNOW?

Quarter horses exist in all solid colors. The majority of them are chestnut.

The quarter horse came from Spanish origins, like these Andalusians.

MORGAN

All modern-day Morgans are related to a single stallion named Justin Morgan. Justin Morgan was born in Massachusetts in 1789. He became legendary in his time for his unmatched strength and stamina.

Today's Morgans display the same strength and stamina that made their forefather famous. These horses are intelligent and spirited, but easy to control and gentle around children. Morgans typically stand between 14.2 and 15.2 hands high. Most have coats that are chestnut, bay, brown, or black in color. They also have silky manes and tails.

Morgans were especially bred for pleasure and have many uses for today's horse enthusiasts. Their intelligence and athletic abilities help them excel in competitions such as dressage and endurance riding. Morgans are also an ideal horse for casual trail rides. The Morgan is up to the challenge of almost any activity.

POWERFUL GENES

Most foals display characteristics from both parents. But Justin Morgan's offspring always took after him. Generations of Morgans have continued to pass on the stallion's physical and behavioral traits.

Morgan foal

DID YOU KNOW?

Justin Morgan was originally named Figure. Later he was renamed Justin Morgan after his owner.

Justin Morgan

LIGHTNING-FAST
Thoroughbreds

Known to be the fastest long-distance horse in the world, the Thoroughbred rules the racetrack. This breed's body was made for speed. Long, strong legs provide power. A deep chest allows the horse's lungs to expand when breathing heavily. Physical features like these help the Thoroughbred reach speeds of 43 miles (69 km) per hour.

ARABIAN INFLUENCE

Thoroughbreds were developed in England about 300 years ago with three Arabian sires. These Arabians were the Byerley Turk, the Darley Arabian, and the Godolphin Arabian.

The Thoroughbred's speed is matched by a fiery spirit. In fact some Thoroughbreds have rather challenging temperaments. These horses are extremely courageous and bold. Though sometimes difficult to control, their daring natures can be an advantage on the racetrack.

Thoroughbreds are not only renowned for their speed and spirit, but also for their beauty. Most Thoroughbreds stand 16 to 16.2 hands high. Their shiny coats are generally brown, chestnut, black, or gray. They currently reign as one of the world's most popular breeds.

PATTERNED *Beauties*

Some horse breeds are known for their strength or speed. But the Appaloosa and paint horse are known for their colorful coats. Both of these breeds come from horses brought to America by Spanish explorers. American Indians are responsible for developing the two breeds.

The Appaloosa and paint horse have many similarities. Both have compact bodies and strong muscles built for power. But differences exist between the two breeds.

THE NAME GAME

When different groups of people first saw horses, they needed names to describe them. American Indians came up with "big dog," "holy dog," and "elk dog." Hawaiians called horses "canoes that travel on land." Australians called them "the newcomer's kangaroo."

DID YOU KNOW?

A horse was once a sign of wealth among American Indian tribes.

Most Appaloosas are slightly smaller than the average paint horse. They also have thin, wispy manes. They are extremely intelligent but prone to stubbornness. Paint horses are calm and easygoing.

For American Indians, it was the Appaloosa and paint horse's patterned coats that made them especially valuable. The patterns helped these horses blend in with their surroundings. American Indians riding paint horses or Appaloosas could better sneak up on their enemies. Today both breeds make the list of America's top 10 most popular horse breeds.

APPALOOSA

Appaloosa fans can thank the Nez Perce tribe for the creation of this colorful breed. The Nez Perce lived in the Pacific Northwest. They began breeding Appaloosas in the 1700s. Tribe members needed a horse that could handle long hunts and mountainous terrain. They bred Appaloosas to be intelligent, sensible, and athletic. These traits, along with the Appaloosa's beautiful coat, make them popular horses today.

The Appaloosa's athletic abilities help it excel in both jumping and racing. Thanks to their striking appearance, many Appaloosas have even appeared in circuses and parades. This is one horse that truly has the best of both worlds—beauty and brains.

COOL COATS

Appaloosas have five different coat patterns.

snowflake

white spots on the
body and hips

blanket

white on the hips, with
or without dark spots

leopard

white on the sides and
hips with dark spots

frost

white flecks on
a dark coat

marble

light coat covered
with dark flecks

Palouse River in Washington

DID YOU KNOW?

Appaloosas are named
after the Palouse River.
This river runs through
the states of Washington
and Idaho, where the
Nez Perce once lived.

PAINT Horse

It's easy to see how the paint horse got its name. These horses look as if a bucket of paint was splashed on their bodies. Unlike the Appaloosa, which has small speckles, the paint horse has large patches of color.

The most common type of coloring for a paint horse is tobiano. Tobiano horses have white coats with dark patches. Overo horses have dark coats with white patches. Sabino is a special term for horses that have white markings starting on their legs and running up their bodies. Splashed white describes paint horses that are largely covered in white with dark patches that have smooth edges.

American Indians living in the central plains brought this breed fame. Soon cowboys and pioneers also fell in love with the paint horse's calm and steady nature. This horse is happy just about anywhere, whether on the trail or in the ring.

PINTO VS. PAINT

Many people think pintos and paint horses are the same breed. But the pinto isn't a breed at all. A pinto is any horse with a two-colored coat. Paint horses, however, must meet actual breed standards.

DID YOU KNOW?

A paint horse's skin has the same color patches as its coat.

47

HEAVY *Lifters*

About 1,500 years ago, a Chinese invention forever changed the lives of horses and humans. The invention was a padded collar that could be placed around a horse's neck. With these collars horses could be used to pull wagons, plows, and timber. Forests could be cleared faster than ever before, and farmers were able to harvest more crops.

But not just any horse could be used to pull such heavy loads. Only the world's strongest, heaviest, and most powerful horses were equipped for such tasks. Two of these horses are still famous today—the Percheron and the Clydesdale.

MACHINES TAKE THE REINS

By the 1950s and 1960s, machines had replaced almost all of the heavy horses' jobs. The demand for heavy horses plummeted. Some heavy horse breeds nearly became extinct.

DID YOU KNOW?

Heavy horse breeds such as the Suffolk are still struggling to regain their numbers.

Suffolk

PERCHERON

The Percheron was developed in France and is known as one of the world's most versatile breeds. Gifted with incredible strength, Percherons are ideal horses for pulling heavy farm equipment. But that's not all these horses can do. They have also been used as warhorses and coach horses. Percherons have even been saddled up and ridden for pleasure. Their grace, intelligence, and calm temperaments make Percherons suitable for many different purposes.

Percherons stand between 16 and 17.2 hands high. They have deep chests and extremely muscular legs. Most Percherons are gray or black with thick manes. These hardy, easygoing giants are extremely popular. They have been sold all over the world.

A BIG DEAL

"DR. LeGEAR
THE GIANT HORSE

The largest Percheron on record was named Dr. LeGear. Born in 1902 Dr. LeGear stood 21 hands high and weighed 3,024 pounds (1,372 kilograms). The world record for the smallest horse goes to Thumbelina, a miniature horse that stands 4.4 hands high and weighs 57 pounds (26 kg).

DID YOU KNOW?

Oriental and Spanish breeds were used to develop the Percheron. These breeds gave the Percheron its elegance and grace.

CLYDESDALE

Percherons may be one of the world's most versatile horses, but Clydesdales are the world's strongest. This breed was developed during the 1700s in Scotland by the sixth Duke of Hamilton and John Paterson. Both Flemish horses and Shires were used to develop the Clydesdale.

DID YOU KNOW?

A single Clydesdale once pulled a 50-ton (45-metric ton) load across a distance of 1,320 feet (402 meters)!

Clydesdales measure up to 16.2 hands high. Most are bay, brown, or black. Many have white markings on their legs and face, with heavy feathering on their large, broad hooves. They are recognized as friendly horses that are eager to please and quick to learn.

In the 1700s and 1800s, Clydesdales were used to pull heavy farm equipment in Great Britain. Like Percherons, they were so good at pulling heavy loads that they were sold all over the world. They are surprisingly active for their large size and have elegant ways of moving. Today Clydesdales are often seen pulling carriages in parades.

EQUINE QUIZ

How well do you know your horse breeds? Take this quiz to find out.

1. _____ are the world's fastest long-distance racehorses.
   a. Morgans
   b. Thoroughbreds
   c. quarter horses
   d. Percherons

2. The Nez Perce tribe is responsible for developing the_____.
   a. paint horse
   b. quarter horse
   c. Appaloosa
   d. Morgan

5. The biggest_____ on record was born in 1902 and named Dr. LeGear.
   a. Clydesdale
   b. Percheron
   c. quarter horse
   d. Morgan

3. The_____ is named for the quarter-mile races it once competed in.
   a. Clydesdale
   b. paint horse
   c. Percheron
   d. quarter horse

4. Tobiano and overo are coat patterns for the_____.
   a. Thoroughbred
   b. Clydesdale
   c. Morgan
   d. paint horse

6. Justin Morgan is the sire responsible for today's_____.
   a. Thoroughbreds
   b. paint horses
   c. Morgans
   d. Appaloosas

7. Because of their extreme pulling abilities,_____were once sold all over the world.
   a. Clydesdales
   b. paint horses
   c. Thoroughbreds
   d. quarter horses

SADDLE Up!

RIDING *a Horse*

Does the thought of riding a horse make you think of freedom, speed, or grace? You're not alone. Horses have shaped history for thousands of years. Before the invention of the automobile and railroads, people depended on horses for all sorts of things. Soldiers relied on horses in war times. The postal service delivered mail on horseback. Farmers used horses to plow fields and haul heavy loads. Horse-drawn carriages and wagons did the work of today's cars, trucks, ambulances, taxis, and more. Today most American horses are considered family pets, ranch horses, or show partners.

HORSES RESOURCES

Horse lovers eager to get in the saddle can learn more by reading books about riding. There are also good horse training videos and TV shows available. If there's a stable nearby, volunteer with a horse trainer or take riding lessons. You can also look online to find a 4-H club near you or join the U.S. Pony Club. Your county's extension office might also have information about horsemanship camps.

DID YOU KNOW?

The Women's Professional Rodeo Association has over 2,500 members. It is the oldest women's sport association in the United States.

JUST WHAT THE DOCTOR ORDERED

Scientists have proven what horse lovers have known for some time—being around horses makes people happy. It's no wonder horses make great therapy animals. Hospital patients can benefit from a friendly visit from a specially trained miniature horse. Some minis are even trained as guide animals for people with vision problems.

Doctors and physical therapists can include horses in therapy treatments for people with injuries, disabilities, or emotional problems. This is called hippotherapy. Hippotherapy uses the rhythm and repetition of horse riding to increase a patient's muscle strength, balance, and flexibility.

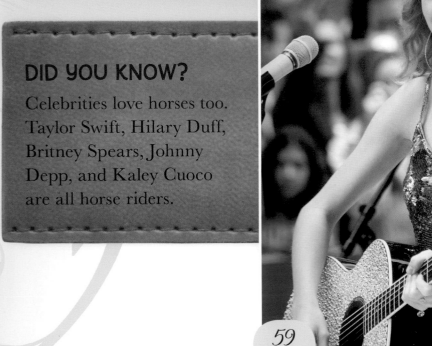

DID YOU KNOW?

Celebrities love horses too. Taylor Swift, Hilary Duff, Britney Spears, Johnny Depp, and Kaley Cuoco are all horse riders.

Taylor Swift

TWO-LEGGED FOUR-LEGGED *and Athletes*

Horse riding is a sport, and a horse and rider are athletes. Riders need good posture, balance, and strength in the saddle. Riding a horse is great exercise. People interested in riding should stay active or get involved in team sports. Regular exercise builds strength needed to be a good rider.

It's best to choose a riding style and competition that fits both horse and rider. Are you good at some activities but not so good at others? Horses are the same way. A shorter horse may not be cut out for jumping. A horse that isn't flexible won't do well in dressage. A horse that gets scared easily probably won't make a good competitive trail horse. A horse with a slow, laid-back personality is probably not right for speed events like barrel racing. If you plan to compete, remember that it takes practice, patience, and time to become a winning team.

polo

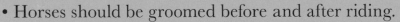

SAFE RIDING TIPS

Here are some tips to remember before riding a horse.
• Always ride with adult supervision.
• Horse and rider should warm up before riding.
• Always wear a safety helmet and boots.
• Only use riding equipment that is in good, clean condition.
• Horses should be groomed before and after riding.
• Watch for holes or obstacles on the ground that could cause a horse to stumble.
• Never ride in the dark.
• Don't startle a horse from behind—they may kick.

DID YOU KNOW?

It's important to start a new exercise routine slowly to avoid injury.

Riding TACK

The equipment used for horseback riding is called tack. Basic tack includes a saddle and a bridle. Western and English saddles sit right behind the horse's shoulder blades, on saddle pads. The saddles are designed to spread the rider's weight evenly across the horse's back. They are secured with a girth, which is a strap that stretches under the narrowest part of a horse's belly. Just like people, each horse has a different body shape. It's important to choose a saddle that fits a horse's shape.

It's also important to choose a bridle that fits. A bridle is like a horse's headgear. It holds a metal bit in the horse's mouth. The rider uses reins attached to the bit to guide the horse.

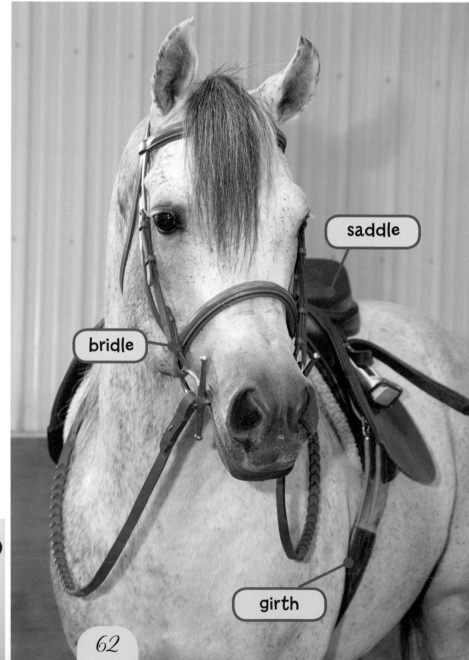

saddle

bridle

girth

SLOW TO SPEEDY: RIDING GAITS

The speed of a horse is called a gait. There are different gaits for English and Western riding.

ENGLISH

walk—a relaxed pace
trot—faster than the Western jog; it's too bumpy for a rider to sit comfortably. Instead the rider rises out of the saddle in rhythm with the horse.
canter—the English version of the Western lope
gallop—the horse takes longer steps than in a lope or canter but moves slower than when it's running

WESTERN

walk—a relaxed pace
jog—the horse takes longer steps to cover more ground; the rider still sits comfortably in the saddle
lope—faster than a trot but slower than a gallop
gallop—the horse takes longer steps than in a lope or canter but moves slower than when it's running

trot

WESTERN
Riding Competitions

A rider who daydreams about ranch life as an American cowgirl or cowboy might enjoy Western riding. These ranchers take care of wounded animals, move herds of cattle, repair fences, and check food and water in all types of weather. Western riders need a calm, comfortable, quick horse. Today there are riding competitions that test the kind of horse-rider teamwork needed on a ranch.

COWGIRL COMFORT

Ranchers can spend days or even weeks in the saddle, tending to livestock. The deep seat and long stirrups of a Western saddle are comfortable for long rides.

Today's Western saddles are specialized for different riding events. Show saddles and bridles often have fancy silver trimmings. For most Western horse show events, riders wear long-sleeved shirts, jeans, boots, and Western hats. Chaps are also stylish.

DID YOU KNOW?

A rider traditionally mounts a horse from the left side. This dates back to a time when ancient soldiers first rode horses into battle. Right-handed warriors carried their swords on their left hips. Mounting from the left kept riders from injuring their horses— or stabbing themselves in the foot!

CUTTING
Competitions

Sometimes ranchers need to separate, or cut, a cow from a large herd. This is done to give the cow medicine or treat an injury. This basic ranch duty led to cutting competitions. It takes an advanced rider with a horse that's trained around cows to compete.

In cutting competitions a small herd of cattle is gathered at one end of an arena. Competitors ride quietly into the herd and push one cow away. Like a soccer goalie watching the opposing team, a cutting horse is trained to predict a cow's movements. When the cow tries to run back to the herd, the horse crouches low and moves quickly. If the cow moves too fast, the horse spins around and runs to block it. Horse and rider must keep the cow away from the herd for 2.5 minutes.

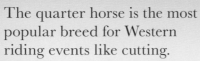

The quarter horse is the most popular breed for Western riding events like cutting.

Barrel RACING

DID YOU KNOW?
The fastest barrel racers have completed the cloverleaf pattern in less than 13.5 seconds.

Barrel racing began in Texas and gave women a rodeo sport all their own. Today men are barrel racers too, but girls still rule the sport.

This might be the right sport for a rider who likes speed. Barrel racers enter the competition arena at a full run. They aim for three large barrels arranged in a triangle. The goal is to race in a cloverleaf pattern around the barrels without knocking one over. It takes practice to make tight turns around each barrel and then regain full speed in about two steps. If a barrel is knocked over, there is a time penalty. At the end of the event, the rider with the fastest time wins.

DID YOU KNOW?

Horses that compete in barrel racing, cutting, jumping, and other active events wear protective leg wraps or boots.

Trail RIDING

For riders who like obstacle courses, trail competitions might be a perfect fit. Riders are judged on their ability to maneuver their horses through patterns of difficult challenges. Horses are judged on agility, willingness, and calmness.

The pattern isn't announced until the morning of the event, so riders have to memorize it quickly. Horse and rider must work as a team. Patterns might call for competitors to jog over logs, cross a wooden bridge, or slosh through water. A trail horse can't get scared if a rider is asked to pick up a noisy tarp, rattle a can of pebbles, or pull a strange object out of a mailbox. Points are deducted if the pattern is not completed or if obstacles are knocked over.

ENGLISH
Riding Competitions

English riding may be a great choice for people who want to ride horses like British royalty. This riding style began long ago in the European military. It later became the preferred style for English fox hunting and racing sports. It is still a formal style of riding. Today there are many English riding competitions to choose from.

PETITE SEAT

The small English saddles were designed to allow horses better movement at different speeds and over jumps. They come in different styles for events like dressage, jumping, and polo. Riders using English saddles have closer leg contact with their horses. The shorter stirrups allow the rider to rise out of the saddle in rhythm with the horse's trot. This up and down motion is called posting.

For competitions a rider wears a show jacket called a hunt coat, as well as breeches, riding boots, and a helmet. Some events require gloves too. A rider's hair must be above the collar. English bridles have a simple bit.

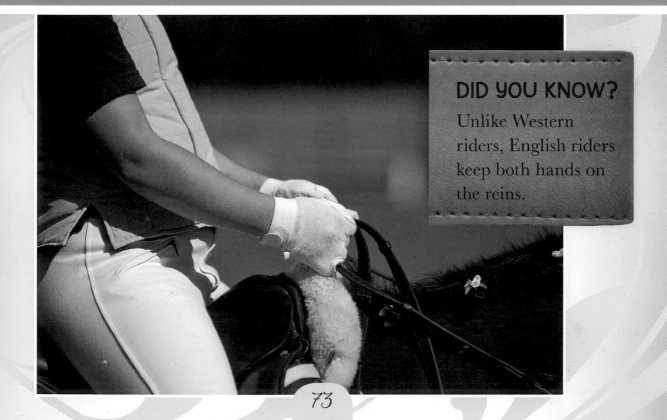

DID YOU KNOW?

Unlike Western riders, English riders keep both hands on the reins.

Show JUMPING

Show jumping is like jumping hurdles at a track meet. Horses must have long, lean bodies, good jumping instincts, and powerful legs. There are jumping classes for ponies too.

Riders sit in a position called forward seat. Riders keep their backs straight and bend their legs, so their hips are directly above their ankles. They must keep their weight balanced in both stirrups. If they lose their balance, riders can fall off. A rider shifts his or her weight out of the saddle, just as the horse lifts off the ground to jump. This relieves the weight from the horse's back.

Competitions take place in an arena with a pattern of colorful hurdles that look like fences. In addition to clearing the hurdles, competitors may have to jump two rails instead of one or leap over a pool of water.

Some professional show jumpers can clear hurdles that are 7 feet (2.1 m) high.

DID YOU KNOW?

Three English riding events are part of the Olympic games—show jumping, dressage, and eventing. Eventing is like a triathlon, where riders compete in dressage, show jumping, and cross-country riding.

DRESSAGE

Riders who enjoy gymnastics or ballet may like dressage. Dressage is a French word that means training, but it should mean dancing. Horses are taught to change the length of their steps and flex their necks and bodies. Their movements look like a dance. Horses can trot and canter in one spot, spin on one foot, or extend their gaits to look like they are floating. The most experienced dressage horses can even learn fancy kicks.

PASSING THE TEST

Many people consider dressage the highest form of horse training. It can take eight or nine years for a horse and rider to pass through the nine training levels of dressage. To advance to the next training level, horse and rider must pass tests at competitions.

At dressage competitions, horse and rider teams perform alone in an arena. Lettered markers are placed around the arena to mark where certain gait changes or movements are required. Riders and their horses must perform each skill at the designated markers.

DRESSING UP FOR DRESSAGE

A dressage rider wears a long, dark riding jacket, white shirt, white tie, white or tan breeches, black boots, white gloves, and a helmet or top hat. The saddle is wider and has longer stirrups.

A horse's mane and tail are braided for dressage competitions. Tiny braids are often folded into little balls, forming button braids.

DID YOU KNOW?

Before beginning a performance, a dressage competitor must nod to the judge in a salute. He or she must salute before leaving the arena as well.

Horse RACING

10   **9**   **8**   **7**   **6**   **5**

Horse racing competitions have been around for as long as people have ridden horses. The muscular quarter horse is the fastest breed in shorter races. They can run .25 miles (.4 km) in less than 21 seconds. But the long, lean body of the Thoroughbred makes it the fastest breed for long distance races. On race day horses are loaded into the starting stalls on the racetrack. The starting gate opens and the horses bolt forward, starting the clock.

The race is on!

Jockeys ride racehorses. They wear race uniforms called silks. Unlike most athletes, jockeys must be strong but small. There are strict rules about how much weight a racehorse is allowed to carry. Some races allow no more than 110 pounds (50 kg) total, including the saddle. Luckily racing saddles weigh little more than 1 pound (.5 kg). If the jockey and saddle don't weigh enough, weighted saddle pads are added.

OFF TO THE RACES

The Kentucky Derby is the best-known Thoroughbred race. The annual 1.25-mile (2-km) race is called "the most exciting two minutes in sports." If a horse wins the Kentucky Derby, the Preakness Stakes, and the Belmont Stakes, they win the Triple Crown. So far only 11 horses have ever won the Triple Crown.

Secretariat won the Triple Crown in 1973.

TEST YOUR HORSE RIDING IQ

1. If you want to ride like a cowboy, which riding style would you choose?
   a. dressage
   b. English
   c. Western

2. Which event includes an obstacle course?
   a. trail
   b. dressage
   c. cutting
   d. barrel racing

3. Which speed event class was created for girls?
   a. horse racing
   b. show jumping
   c. dressage
   d. barrel racing

4. Which event takes years to master and looks like a dance?
a. barrel racing
b. dressage
c. trail
d. cutting

5. Which of the following is a safe riding tip?
a. pack snacks
b. never sneak up on a horse from behind
c. ride with adult supervision
d. B and C

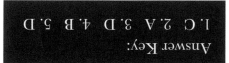

Answer Key:
1.C 2.A 3.D 4.B 5.D

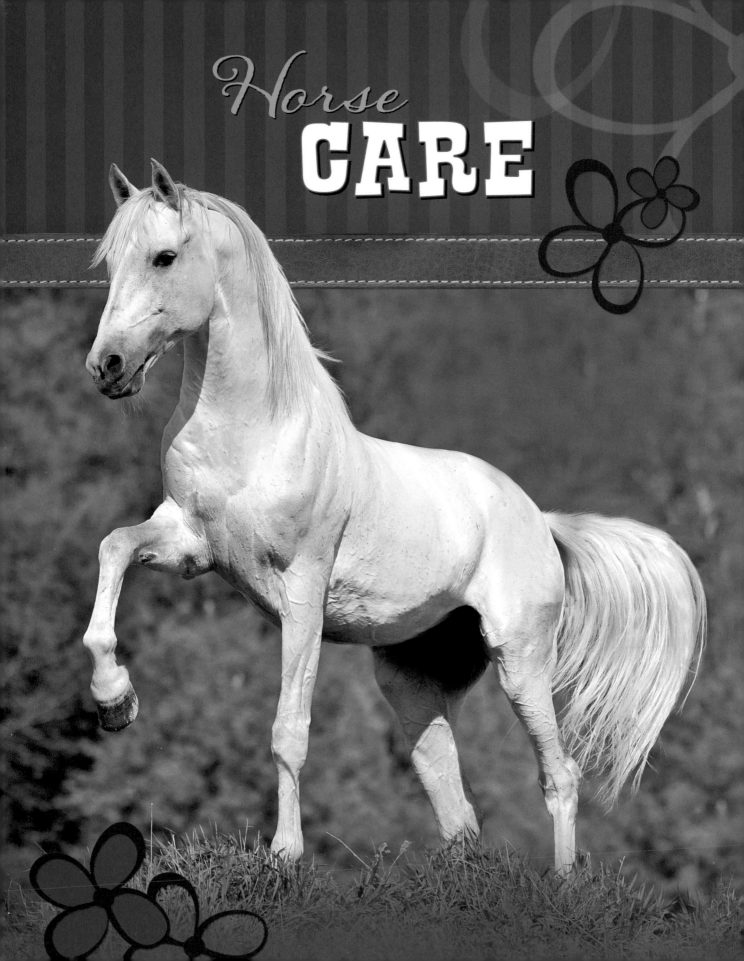

Horse
CARE

Our LARGEST Pets

Are you crazy about horses? You're not alone. People have had a special relationship with horses for centuries. There are an estimated 58 million horses in the world, and most of them are pets. That's a lot of horses for girls to love. Learning to take care of these large pets is a big responsibility.

HOME *for a* HORSE

The ideal home for a horse is in a safe pasture with other horses. This open, grassy area should have strong fences and gates. Fences and gates should be made from materials that are safe for horses. Barbed wire should never be used. The sharp barbs on the wire fencing can cause serious injuries. Pastures should have lots of healthy grass. There also needs to be a shelter to protect against bad weather. Trees can shade a horse from the summer sun, but they can't protect against wind, rain, snow, and hail. For horses that aren't kept in stables, a three-sided shed that faces away from the worst winds is ideal.

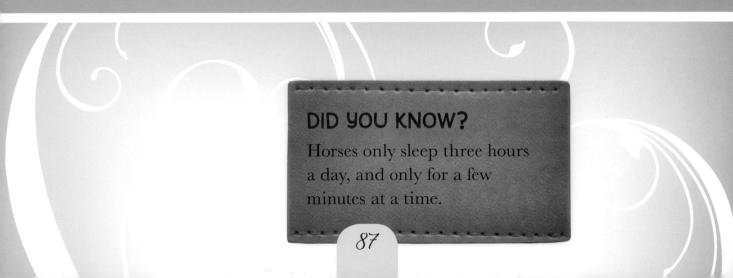

A SAFE SPACE

Horse owners should inspect the area before their horses move in. They should remove things like trash, nails, soda cans, broken glass, and loose wire. If a horse eats poisonous weeds, it can become very sick. These should also be removed.

DID YOU KNOW?

Horses only sleep three hours a day, and only for a few minutes at a time.

A ROOM with a VIEW

Boarding stables rent space for horses. Many stable owners agree to feed these horses when owners can't. In herds horses always stick together in small groups. So it's best to look for a stable that boards several horses.

Stables should be well built with plenty of ventilation for clean air and good drainage to keep floors dry. Check for sharp edges or nails that could hurt the horse. Make sure the horse has at least a 12-by-12-foot (3.6-by-3.6-m) stall, to allow plenty of space to move around. Safe bedding for the floor keeps horses comfortable and dry. Wood shavings, straw, and rubber mats are good options.

HORSE CARE IS A DIRTY JOB

A horse can produce up to 50 pounds (23 kg) of manure every day. So it's important to clean, or muck, horse stalls daily. Horse owners should keep a stall fork, shovel, wheelbarrow, and broom handy. They should wear boots and an old pair of jeans for the dirtiest work of horse care.

DID YOU KNOW?

Many stables have outdoor runs attached to stalls. These runs are like tiny yards.

HUNGRY *Horses*

Horses are built to graze on grass all day and night. This constant walking to find food gives them lots of exercise. You might say horses are munching athletes.

Hay is the next best thing to grass, but sometimes horses need grain too. Grain is a good option for stabled horses that don't have access to grass. Grain also can provide extra nutrition for older horses and extra calories for work and show horses.

The climate, a horse's age, weight, and activity level will help determine the amount and type of food it needs. There are many kinds of horse feed available. Horse owners should ask a veterinarian or horse care expert about the best diet for their horses.

DID YOU KNOW?

The average 1,000-pound (454-kg) horse eats about 25 pounds (11 kg) of food a day. Most of that should come from grass or hay.

Owners of older horses may need to soak food in water first. This softens the food, making it easier for older horses to eat.

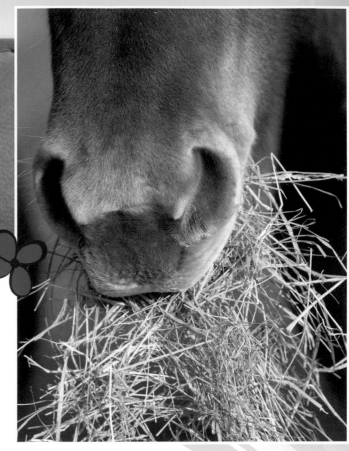

A SWEET TREAT

Occasionally it's OK for horses to have a special treat. Stick to natural foods like apples or carrots. But remember too many treats can upset a horse's stomach.

Sticky Horse Treats

Coat a carrot or half an apple in corn syrup. Cover with dry oats to make a healthy horse snack.

GULP, GULP, GULP

Horses need lots of water to stay healthy. You'd be thirsty too if you ate that much dry food. Horses can drink up to 20 gallons (76 liters) of water every day. Ponds, lakes, or other natural water sources usually provide safe drinking water for horses. If water troughs or buckets are used, it is important to keep them clean and full of fresh water to avoid bacteria.

WINTER WOES

On cold winter days, it's nice to be warm and cozy inside. But horse owners can't get too comfy. They must care for their horses in all types of weather. Here are some winter tips to keep horses safe.

❇ Check water buckets and troughs several times a day to be sure the horse's water hasn't frozen. Consider using heated buckets and water troughs.

❇ Ask a veterinarian about increasing hay or grain during winter months. A horse may need the extra calories to stay warm.

❇ Provide shelter from the wind, rain, and snow.

❇ A horse's fuzzy winter coat may not be enough to keep it warm when it's cold out. A horse blanket might be necessary.

❇ Don't stop spending time with a horse just because it's cold. A horse needs attention and exercise during the winter too.

DID YOU KNOW?

Daylight controls when a horse grows its fuzzy coat. Shorter fall and winter days work like a natural timer, signaling a wardrobe change to a thicker coat.

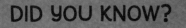

EXERCISE

Imagine being cooped up in your bedroom all day and night. You would go stir crazy. A horse doesn't want to be stuck in a stall all day either. Horses are built to move. They need 30 to 60 minutes of exercise most days of the week.

Most horses need free time in a pasture or arena. They can kick up their heels, run, and wander freely. It is the ultimate recess time. When a horse is cooped up in a stall, keep it entertained with special horse toys like giant balls and knotted ropes. Some racehorses and show horses even go swimming in special pools or use horse-sized treadmills to stay in shape.

LONGE LINE

Using a longe line lets a horse get exercise in a controlled environment. The horse is attached to a 20- to 30-foot (6.1- to 9.1-m) longe line that the owner holds. The horse moves in a wide circle around its owner. A horse can learn to longe by making small circles during walks. With a little practice, the horse can learn to change speed with different vocal commands.

DID YOU KNOW?

In the wild, horses can walk up to 50 miles (80 km) a day.

GET BACK in the SADDLE

Horse riding is great exercise for the horse and rider. It's also a fun way to learn and explore areas together. Riders can go on trails or through large fields. They can also get involved in horse shows.

BEWARE OF THE KICK!

In the wild good eyesight helps horses detect predators. If they are startled or feel threatened, horses can send a powerful kick. Stay safe and never sneak up behind a horse.

DID YOU KNOW?

Horses can see almost directly behind them.

HORSE *Grooming*

Grooming a horse is a good way to create a special bond while keeping the horse looking great. Before reaching for a saddle, a rider should always groom his or her horse to make sure dirt and burrs aren't rubbing against it. Grooming is the perfect time to check for health concerns too. In herds horses regularly groom each other with their teeth. Thankfully people just need some basic tools.

Coat Brushes

Unlike your hair, a horse's coat doesn't need to be brushed every day unless it's really messy. But most horses like being brushed. There are stiff-bristled brushes, used for thicker coats or when there's lots of dirt. There are also soft bristle brushes for polishing shorter coats. A rubber curry comb can remove dried mud and loose hair. Rubbing the curry in a circular motion feels like a massage to a horse.

DID YOU KNOW?

A dirty horse can be a good thing. That dirt is natural protection against sun, water, and insects.

Manes and Tails

Long, short, curly, straight—there are all kinds of manes and tails. While grooming a horse, don't forget to tackle tangles and burrs. A wide-toothed comb or stiff brush will do the trick. Tangle-free tails are important because they act as a horse's built-in fly swatter.

Bathing

Many horses like to be rinsed off in hot weather, but they rarely need soapy baths. When preparing for summertime competitions, riders may decide to break out the horse shampoo. Give the horse a chance to get used to the water by getting its legs wet first. A horse doesn't like to get its head wet, so use a damp sponge to wash that adorable face.

BRAIDING BREEDS

There are different mane and tail style options for horse competitions.

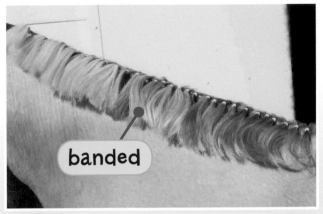

banded

roached

banded—tiny ponytails in the mane that lay flat against the neck

plaited—braiding or weaving designs in a horse's mane

plaited tail—the hair is French braided and goes three-fourths of the way down the tailbone

roached—manes that are shaved to look like a man's crew cut

banged—the end of a long tail is trimmed straight across

DID YOU KNOW?

Braiding a horse's tail when it's wet can create a wavy look after it dries.

HEALTHY *Hooves*

FROG

Horses can't survive without four hooves to support their weight. Hooves are made of layers of thick protein called keratin, just like your fingernails. In the middle of the hoof, there is a triangle-shaped cushion under the heel called a frog. The frog is especially sensitive to stones and hard dirt. A hoof pick is used to safely clean hooves from heel to toe.

When your fingernails get too long, you can trim them with nail clippers and a file. Every six weeks a horse's hooves need to be trimmed by a farrier. These professionals care for hooves. Farriers will keep hooves the right length to prevent cracking. They use hoof-sized clippers called nippers. Farriers also use large nail files called rasps. If a horse needs horseshoes, the farrier knows how to shape and attach them properly. One set of shoes should last a horse for six weeks.

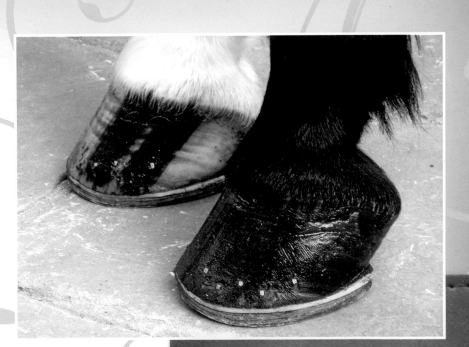

DID YOU KNOW?

Show horses can wear clear or black hoof polish for special events.

Pearly WHITES

Losing a baby tooth is a big deal. Horses have baby teeth too. It takes about 4.5 years for a horse to lose its last baby tooth. By then it has 36 to 44 permanent teeth. But those teeth continue to grow throughout a horse's life. In the wild, grazing helps a horse's teeth stay smooth and healthy. But a domestic horse's diet isn't the same as a wild horse. Sometimes its upper and lower teeth can rub against each other, filing them into sharp points that look like fangs. Imagine not being able to eat because sharp teeth cut into your cheeks, gums, or tongue. Ouch!

Not eating can lead to malnutrition. This is especially a problem with older horses. An equine dentist can file down sharp points with a dental rasp. They watch for other mouth problems too. Equine dentists are veterinarians who receive special training to take care of a horse's teeth. It's a good idea for a horse to get a dental checkup at least once a year.

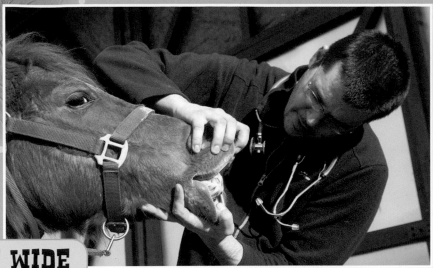

OPEN WIDE

You can't ask a horse to climb into a dentist's chair and open wide. Usually the dentist will give the horse medicine to help it relax for the exam. A special brace called a speculum keeps its mouth open while the dentist works. Many of their tools are just like the ones your dentist uses—only larger. Dentists look for gum disease, decay, and broken or loose teeth. They also check the horse's ability to chew. After a dental appointment, a horse needs a break from riding for a day or two.

DID YOU KNOW?

Professionals can estimate a horse's age by the amount of wear on its teeth.

HORSE *Health*

Keeping this four-legged friend healthy as a horse requires constant care and regular checkups with a veterinarian. A veterinarian can give horses their required vaccinations and teach owners how to treat for parasites.

But getting a horse to a vet can be a big challenge. Many horse vets will come right to the barn or stable. Their trucks are stocked like an animal clinic on wheels.

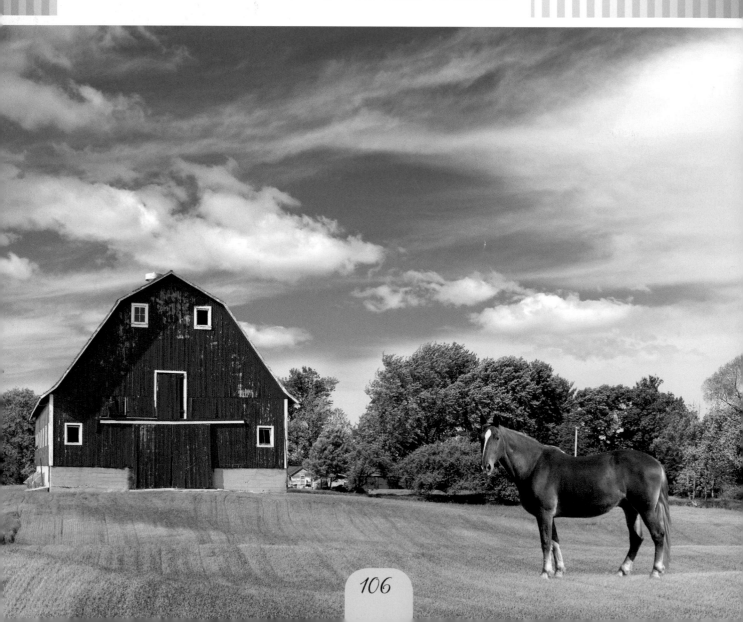

WHEN TO CALL A VETERINARIAN

Horses can't tell you when they're feeling sick, so how do owners know when to call the vet? Sometimes, it's as easy as ABC.

Appearance—Does the horse look like its normal self? Does it have a runny nose, an open wound, or a new limp?

Behavior—How is the horse acting? Is it grouchy or sleepy? Is it eating and drinking well?

Condition—Are there any changes in the horse's weight or to its coat?

STABLE FIRST-AID

Every stable and horse owner should have a first-aid kit. They can be purchased, or people can make a basic kit themselves. Some things that should be included are:

❏ phone numbers of at least two veterinarians
❏ small flashlight
❏ hand sanitizer
❏ detergent; dish soap will work
❏ non-latex gloves
❏ petroleum jelly
❏ scissors
❏ bandages of different sizes
❏ antibiotic ointment
❏ leg wraps
❏ rolled cotton
❏ hydrogen peroxide
❏ rubbing alcohol
❏ large-dose syringe

TEST YOUR HORSE CARE IQ

1. A horse's favorite home would be _____ ?

a. a small stall

b. a safe pasture with a shelter

c. your backyard

2. The amount and type of feed a horse needs depends on _____.

a. the horse's age, weight, and activity level

b. how hungry it is

c. which brand costs less

3. How much water does a horse drink every day?

a. one cup (.2 L)

b. 12 to 20 gallons (45 to 76 L)

c. 10,000 gallons (38,000 L)

4. What kind of fencing should be avoided?

a. barbed wire

b. pole fencing

c. wood fencing

5. How often should a horse's hooves be trimmed?

a. once a week
b. every six weeks
c. once a year

6. A vet should be called if there is a change in a horse's _____.

a. appearance
b. behavior
c. condition
d. all of the above

Snap Books are published by Capstone Press,
1710 Roe Crest Drive, North Mankato, Minnesota 56003
www.capstonepub.com

Library of Congress Cataloging-in-Publication Data
Cataloging-in-publication information is on file with the Library of Congress.
ISBN 978-1-4914-0713-4 (paperback) 978-1-4914-7113-5 (paperback)

Editorial Credits
Michelle Hasselius, editor; Juliette Peters, designer; Deirdre Barton,
media researcher, Laura Manthe, production specialist

Photo Credits
© Mark J. Barrett, 38, 39(top); American Morgan Horse Association, 39 (bottom);
Capstone Studio: Karon Dubke: 29(b), 62, 63, 68, 89(t); Center for American
History, UT Austin: Heinrick Harder Art: 9(t); CLiX Photography: Shawn
Hamilton, 67(t), 70, 75(all), 79(t), 95(t), 101(b); Corbis: Bettmann, 28, 81; Courtesy
of Rural Heritage, 51(t); Getty Images Inc: Boston Globe/Jessica Rinaldi, 59(t),
and, 37; Highland Photography by Darcie Strobach, 71, 77, 78, 82(b); Newscom:
Florilegius, 8; Shutterstock: Abramova Kseniya, cover, 4, 12, 56, acceptphoto, 83(b),
Alexia Khruscheva, 34, 41, Anakondasp, 14, 19(tm), 51(b), Anastasilia Golovokova,
3(br), 7(b), Anastasija Popova, 11(b), 13(bl), 97(b), 109(tl), Ashkabe, 19(tr), AZP
Worldwide, 90, bepsy, 92, Bernd Leitner Fotodesign, 73(b), bikeriderlondon, 60,
Bine, 26, BMJ, 15(tr), Cheryl Ann Quigley, 23(b), Christian Mueller, 20, Clara, 45(b),
103, Claudia Steininger, 17(b), DaCek, 15(bl), De Visu, 65(b), Debby Wong, 59(b),
defotoberg, 24, 82(t), Eastern Light Photography, 19(tl), 85, 91(t), 102, ebubekir
olcok, 54(t), Ekina, 21(bm), elliz, 47(t), Elya Vatel, 58, Eric Isselée, 9(b), 11(t),
107(t), fotoedu, 74, Gail Johnson, 96, Goldika, 108(tr), Goran Bogicevic, 5, Gregory
Johnston, 48(right), gurinaleksandr, 35(t), Hamik, 87, iLiyan, 88, JKlingebiel, 2–3,
johnbraid, 52, Johnny Adolphson, 108(tl), Joy Brown, 99, Joyful, 109(tr), jurra8, 98,
Karen Givens, 100(b), Kenneth Sponsler, 65(t), Kondrashov Mikhail Evgenevich,
76, 83(t), Kotenko Oleksandr, 112, Lenkadan, 15(mr), 36, lightbeserk, 55(t), Lorelei
Girod-b, 21(tr), Makarova Vikoria, 13(tr), 19 (b), 31, 84, Margo Harrison, 53,
Mariait, 10, 15(ml), 16, 21(tm, bl), 27(b), 57, 94, marikond, 69, MaxyM, 106, melis,
105(t), Miao Liao, 86, Myway8, 15(tl), Nate Allred, 91(b), Neale Cousland, 80,
Nicole Ciscato, 18, 21(br), 45(tr), 49(b), Olga_i, 33(t), outdoorsman, 54(b), Papava,
48(l), Paula Cobleigh, 45(b), Pawell Kazmierczak, 109(b), Perry Correll, 50, 79(b),
Peter38, 49(t), pirita, 32(b), 40, Raymond B. Summers, 93(t), Reddogs, 6, Rita
Kochmarjova, 72, 97(t), 104, Robert Hoetink, 95(b), Roynrg, 61, Stefan Holm, 7(tr),
Stephanie Coffman, 89(b), StudioNewmarket, 29(t), Tamara Didenko, 1, 73(t),
Theunis Jacobus Botha, 23(t), Thirteen, 13(br), Thitisan krobkham, 108(b), Todd
Klassy, 64, Tom Plesnik: 25, Tomashko, 105(b), TTStudio, 100(t), Vanessa Nel, 66,
Vera Zinkova, 45(mr), 67(b), Vespa, 27(t), Volker Rauch, 101(tr), vovabryzgin, 110,
VVO, 107(b), Winthrop Brookhouse, 35(b), YanLev, 22, Zuzule, 13(tl), 17(t), 21(tl),
30, 32(t), 33(b), 42, 43, 44, 45(tm, tl, ml), 46, 47(b), 55(b), 93(b); Wikipedia, 101(tl),
Horsemanship for Woman by Theodore Hoe Mead, 7(tl). All design elements are
credited to Shutterstock.

Printed in China.
042015   008896R

INDEX